EKPHRASIS AS DIVINATION
AN INCANTATION CATALOGUE

BY ROBYN LEIGH LEAR

INSPIRED BY THE DIVINATORY PLAYING CARDS DESIGNED BY THEO HALL

Ekphrasis as Divination: An Incantation Catalogue
Text Copyright © 2025 Robyn Leigh Lear
Artwork Copyright © 2025 Theo Hall
All Rights Reserved.
Published by Unsolicited Press.
Printed in the United States of America.
First Edition.

No part of this book may be used or reproduced in any manner whatsoever without written permission except in the case of brief quotations embodied in critical articles or reviews. People, places, and notions in these poems are from the author's imagination; any resemblance to real persons or events is purely coincidental.

The artwork graciously donated by Theo Hall is licensed exclusively for this book and may not be copied, reproduced, or excerpted whatsoever unless Unsolicited Press has provided explicit written permission from the artist to the user.

Attention schools and businesses: for discounted copies on large orders, please contact the publisher directly.

For information contact:
Unsolicited Press
Portland, Oregon
www.unsolicitedpress.com
orders@unsolicitedpress.com
619-354-8005

Cover Design: Kathryn Gerhardt
Editor: Summer Stewart

ISBN: 978-1-963115-22-2

To Lance Ümmenhofer
The foundation my dreaming
grows with—and because you see
so deeply into my ghosts

And to Jody Bosza Lear
The muse behind all my work.
Love you, Mom

Preface

"Before I got my eye put out –

I liked as well to see

As other creatures, that have eyes –

And know no other way –

So safer – guess – with just my soul

Opon the window pane

Where other creatures put their eyes –

Incautious –"

       Emily Dickinson, Before I got my eye put out – (336)

  The night my Grandmom found out my mother was pregnant with me, she said she looked up into the night sky and discovered a star was missing and poured a cup of loose-leaf Earl Grey tea into a pristine, white teacup. Her divinatory cup was a gift she won in a beauty contest and was gifted by the queen. My Grandmom wasn't able to carry a child, but she shared her history and herself with my mother so authentically, she became her mother. She was more my grandmother than my father's mother ever wanted to be. Grandmom taught us her secrets and gave us her folklore. I have thought a lot about lineage, given I am the first child of an adopted mother. I still wonder if my Grandmom's lore is my lore or if my mother's biological lore is more mine. I imagine it means that half of me is a blank canvas. When thinking about my relationship to her, I always return to the ocean and magnolia flowers as a metaphor to explain the slippage in my lineage. I grew up near the ocean, and so salt water was the air for me, but when we moved to Georgia, the air became empty. I read stories about magnolia flowers, but I could never smell them until someone said the magnolias are flowering in the air. That's when they became real, and I could actually see and experience them. Perhaps that is what it means to share tradition and family without genetics. Someone teaches you how to smell the magnolia flowers and then you can smell them even if you weren't perfumed by them before your learning was gifted to you. That was my Grandmom as a mother and grandmother. She patiently showed us who we were in her history just as patiently as she waited for me to be born. When my mother went into labor with me, she vowed not to leave her side. Grandmom sat in the hospital—and watched my mother struggle to bring me into the hospital light I fought not to be bathed in even after thirteen hours of active labor.

Vividly I can still see my Grandmom as she watched her tea leaves float through the water in her cup while the steam rose, perfuming the air in a floral rosehip mist of ritual conjuring. She sat, sipped, and stared into the dark waves, liquid cresting a form that was living—the ebb and flow of tide winds weaving around her perfectly curled blonde hair. I see her now, standing at the edge of her salt-weathered porch boards, as she read the remnants of her tea leaves that formed images she learned how to see from her mother, who learned how to read them from her mother. She used to tell me, *The leaves said you would be born in June like me, and only twice did they read July.* How she wanted me to share her birth month, but I fought hard against the traditional gestation most children grow through, and three weeks later, with my arms wrapped around my head, I was born on July 1 at 12:10 am. Water child of wave magic, my Grandmom said she should have known, considering I was always jumping toward the ocean inside my mother. Her stories made me wonder at words, knowing my birth was first seen, not through ultrasonic digital soundscapes but through tea rituals and meditations made over emptiness after nourishment.

My Grandma, from the Kentucky holler, may also have possessed medium sight. She came from the region of Appalachia that most Americans try and pretend isn't there. I have largely erased her from this telling because I am still trying to understand how a woman as cold as her could be my grandmother. I suspect she could see with sight because she had a way of knowing what things meant or would mean someday, and when I was a little girl covered in paint, she looked at me and said, *You are going to be a poet, not a painter, child.* She had a way of talking with her tellings.

Maybe that's when language started moving for me? As an artist, I always got stuck on a work or word, and even as a child predicting songs I had never heard sung to get at the predictability of recycled art, I used to get lost inside what lived between the realm of visual and poetry. The meaning has never lived in the linear spheres that appear on the keyboard, symbols dark and meaningless unless they are deciphered. Reading poetry and seeing art will always be a spiritual ritual—maybe this is why we give our work away. I was no stranger to the role of playing the keeper of secrets and knew not to fear them when they appeared before me. So, on a hot humid night enveloped by navy midnight air and conversation, how to accept another wonder.

Theo Hall, in what I imagine to be a fever dream, has been constructing this myth for over a decade, and when they first met with me to discuss *Young World* and the role I would play in it, I was struck by the expansive universe they created using only ink pens, the memories of Mondrian's vertical lines, a scratched-up deck of cards, their partner Joe Kane's diligent mental note-taking, Kandinsky's color language they had never formally studied but lives within them, their occult curiosity, and the haunted Evangelical memories of a Gothic Kansas past they still fight to understand. I saw so much of them in the cards, but Theo needed help to read them, knowing that when the cards burned during their conceptions, and that Theo was making something not beyond the cards but of them. Theo read me the card's myths while we drank rosé over world building.

Theo explained they had also gifted Meg Wade, a Southern Appalachian witch, prophetess of poems, a deck of cards, in hopes they might speak to her in the language only she and her mother and her mother's mother could know. Wanting to learn and research both the tangible realm of divination as well as the mystical truth that can't be recorded of it, I asked Wade if she would feel comfortable doing a reading of me. She agreed, and I was again seated at a kitchen table in Nashville, TN and gifted the language of future reading. I asked a question without voice and drew three cards:

FUTURE

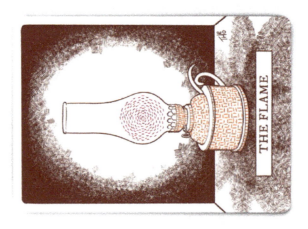

PRESENT

PAST

I watched as Meg unfolded a new sight I had not known I needed to see. I was awestruck at how fluently she could read the symbolic language of Theo's cards because the card's histories have yet to become patterned and expected. She saw into a myth without history, a figurative, playful pack of cards, something I would never have seen or been able to articulate without her guided sight. She read a traumatic past but with the focused certainty of a cat, the animalself—purposeful and specific to the intentions at hand. My past was bleeding into the present, revealed through the closed-eyes smile. The smile, she says, means that your place is beginning, and your goal is to trust the journey. She said it is important that you sit in your trust and follow this new position, be teachable, be present, and relax, knowing your worth, because the future will burn from the fuel of the present you are creating. The flame is the small sun from the many cards sketched by Hall, and while I still struggle to fully articulate this strange moment of intimate transparency, how I cried at Meg's kitchen table because I wasn't ready to be seen as well as she had—I had to admit I found some strange chanting lyric hidden in the card's magic. I didn't want to believe in them, but I did.

I was educated by the mythmaker, baptized by the prophet, and now had to find a historic relevance to ground the poetic voice in before I could write the ekphrastic divination living in the language playing behind the ink in the cards. I turned to Eliot and Kandinsky, knowing they both knew something about the art and the spirit that might lead me into the language of the cards. However, I still did not feel I intimately understood the Tarot tradition to curate a Tarot equivalent, and so I reached out to my dear friend, Ericka Arcadia. She once, while I was making ink paintings, sat next to me at her kitchen table flipping through her own wicked pack of cards, and remarked how every time she plays with them near me, she draws the Empress. She proceeded to interpret why that was strange. Her knowledge and gut always fascinate me—she has a way of braiding fantasies into the most mundane moments—an imagination like hers should be cherished and protected. I asked her to curate the linkage between the young world and old-world cards. I think of her as the historian and know her daydreaming always brings us back to the past when we need to return.

Here is where the poet enters the realm of the mythmaker, prophet, historian, and language weaver. The writing here approaches myth. To do this, I must walk into a chamber adjacent to maiden thought, and I must attempt to erase as much of my ego-self as possible and find the altar, find the mysteries of Modern artists making playful future-telling icons that reflect our generation lost in infinite war and disease, become capable of being in Mystery because they have yet to be discovered by the critics who corrupted our natural child eye, shed and embrace doubt as part of the act of finding, and discard my own need to know truth getting in the way of this language we are creating together. Keats called it negative capability, but I call it, *I with eye*.

If we ever want to achieve ego death, we have to reckon with the recycling of visual traumas we see, our mothers see, our mothers' mothers see throughout our many evolutions of sight. Sight is spiritual, metaphysical, and physical. We have our physical eyes, which are responsible for weaving and constructing a tapestry of experiences that color our world. Our physical eyes are also how we come into language. Then, there are our metaphysical eyes that always perceive our world around us. I will call them childeyes. They know a world we cannot articulate because it is without language. We become a conglomeration of sights here. We know the traumas and joys, the blessings and curses, the pain and the transcendence of our ancestral line within this realm of sight. Then there are our spirit eyes, and we all possess them. I will call them phantom eyes. For those of us who use these eyes, you know who you are—get closer to the *I with eye* construct than I have learned how to define here. To provide a tangible idea to an intangible thought, the phantom eyes are the ones who lead you through the forest at gloaming. They feel when someone is watching you, whether human or not, and you move away from this unwelcome gaze because you felt you saw but didn't see that there was something watching, changed. It is an awareness of how sight is us, how histories of sight is us, and how we must learn not to see through them if we are to find the *I to eye*. Perhaps it is best left defined as an unmapped journey. Here is where we will be when coming to understanding. You must define *the eye and the I* for yourself without the history of haunt tethered to your perception.

When we learn to see through these three eyes and not with them, sight is our sight. To see *is* language and how that builds into using the language of ghosts from the past. Here is where I now divine something between the cards and me, and Arcadia and me, and Wade and me, and Hall and me.

Table of Contents

Preface

Introduction

Notes, *or* **a Key for the Reader to Determine the Singularity in Voice Chorus**

CARD READINGS

Your first reading.
Before We Were Learned We Were Magic

    Follow me in thought, dear reader,   29

    Here is where we renounce consequences.   31

    Poetry is the failed & beautiful expression   33

Your second reading.
What if All I Write and Read is a Nothing and I am a Nothing Too?

    It happened long ago. At the violet hour,   39

    I find that I cannot exist as I look into another   41

    This first book of Nothing looms   43

Your third reading.
Reminiscing Over the Sea

    In the beginning there was nothing,   49

    I am fishing in the dull canal on a winter   51

    We soon forgot we were lost   53

Your fourth reading.
Born to a Cahl: Exploring Our Animalselves

If ever they made a mistake, the river and the trees would bend — 59

She is above all things universal fecundity and the outer sense of — 61

Our strong, intensive interest disappears, — 63

Your fifth reading.
Be Careful What You Read: We Tinker with Sight as Seeing

Imagine Adam's dream— — 69

The whole forest became — 71

Rather than hunger as we do, — 73

Your sixth reading.
Pain is What Doubles Joy

The night of the spirit falls darkly. — 79

I am continually running away from subject— — 81

Art is its intensity. More correctly, — 83

Your seventh reading.
When Someone Told Me a Joke Years Before I Started Listening

The moon pours down influences — 89

The veil or mask   perpetuates change — 91

I have just written my own muse, — 93

Your eighth reading.
I did **do a divination reading for** my **self:**
Death, Corporeal Life, and Destiny

This Threshold is reached by many artificial paths: hash, narcotics, hypnotics of every kind, — 100

The River is my nebulous in-between — 101

Why should we kick against the Pricks — 103

Your ninth reading.
Ode on Writing Divinatory Meanings
I do not look through her glass.   109

Borrow a Botanical Dictionary—turn to the words.   111

Modern artists are beginning to realize   113

Your tenth reading.
What is Beneath / What is Behind / What is Before
They obey Socrates' command—Know thyself.   119

This dual sign is known in very high grades of the Instituted   121

We realized then that the world   123

Your eleventh reading.
Because Their Eyes are Closed
I wrote last of a general weakness   129

Near the Delta where the stream met the sea,   131

Still, we are hiding behind our stoic glare.   133

Your last reading.
Her House: Another Signifier
Every word spoken rouses inner vibrations.   139

We come now to the final practical part,   141

Artists are in every segment.   143

Epilogue,*or* Instructions on How to Reread This Collection should you Choose:

Acknowledgments

About the Makers Behind this Collection

About the Press

Introduction

This collection is composed almost entirely in the form of found language from Theo Hall's writing on the mythos surrounding their deck of fortune-telling cards entitled, *The Young World*. The language used also comes from Kandinsky's *Concerning the Spiritual in Art*, T.S. Eliot's "The Waste Land," Waite's *The Pictorial Key to the Tarot* (written in 1911 and was likely the work Eliot referenced when he was writing "The Waste Land"), and *The Tarot of the Bohemians: The Most Ancient Book in the World, for the Use of Initiates* by Papus (translated by A.P Morton, with the preface written by Waite as well), Keats' Letters, and a few phrases I collected along this journey. Each poem is written in organic form and loosely features three stanzas and a reference to triangles to test the visual theories outlined by Kandinsky on the triangular artistic harmony among creatives. Our triangle is made of the mythmaker, the prophet, and the language weaver.

    I researched the historical traditions and practices of card reading, explored the theoretical and spiritual impact of Hall's divination cards, and then mapped their myths into oracle readings, which were performed for me orally by Meg Wade. This trinity is represented with the three cards used to construct a conduit into meditative poems exploring the limitation of language and art in tandem. This work attempts to marry the three artists' voices into a cohesive conversation that explores the divination of fortune-telling. To limit the scope of this project, Meg Wade read me using only three cards, representing the past, present, and future. To test the theory of divination as ekphrasis, I also included three sections that utilize erasure to construct the verse. This was done to allow the reader to experience the process the poet underwent when divining and constructing the poems themselves as found language divinations. The key for decoding the voices woven together in the collection can be found in the notes section.

Notes,
or a Key for the Reader to Determine the Singularity in Voice Chorus

THE POET // LIQUORISH-COLORED TEXT

When making this collection, I wanted the reader to be able to distinguish between the different voices woven together but did not want the reader to automatically associate with which speaker is the author of the words. Instead, the colors trigger an emotional sensation, the words at time feel familiar, like the memory of a past experience, and lastly, the reader might feel washed by the commonality of human experience and existence. Though the speakers are different, they are all centering around a similar vantage point. Most of this collection is written using found language, but whenever the reader encounters the black text, they know they are reading the poet's self-interjection into the chorus—clarifying the phrasing, defamiliarizing the phrasing, establishing and [re]naming the phrase to connect with the reader of our time. The poet's influence appears as liquorish-colored text.

THE YOUNG WORLD DECK OF CARDS & THEIR MYTHS BY THEO HALL // OCEAN-COLORED TEXT

My friendship with Theo Hall is one of the few treasures I gained during the season of isolation we lived through recently. Their art is playful magic, and I lost myself in the world they constructed. I shared an early draft of this collection with them, and they exclaimed, "Yes! I am blue Jesus!" The joy of seeing their voice in the color-coded poetry tapestry confirmed the pattern I started here. Theo believes the cards "…are not an oracle, though some people have used them as such. They do not claim to be universal archetypes like the Tarot. Rather, they demand that someone recognize them as universal archetypes so that they may change the consciousness of the universe. They are not true, but they want to be true, with all the forcefulness of a confused child. Their oracle abilities have about the same effect. But this does not mean that they do not have their use (just don't try to predict things with them). While not always right, they are as powerfully honest as a child and as powerfully naive. Their absurdity brings into question the absurdity of more grown-up archetypes." Their influence on this work cannot be understated, and I used the color pattern that playfully mimics the red lettering of some versions of the Bible to distinguish between the voices. Their mythic writings appear as ocean-colored text.

Divination Reading on 23 June 2021 by Meg Wade // Appearing in the Whitespace

Meg Wade's language was not used in the construction of these myths, but her spiritual voice was given to me as a beacon to help me navigate the art of divination. Her meditation, her joy, her certainty, and her patience are what helped me craft these readings. In my limited ability and familiarity with the craft of card reading, she became my mother eyes, guiding me into future-telling and meditative manifestations. I then simply had to write her down. Her work appears in the whitespaces.

Concerning the Spiritual in Art by Wassily Kandinsky, translated by M. T. H. Sadler // Amethyst-Colored Text

When preparing for this project, I knew Hall was extremely attracted to the soul-searching of Modernist painters seeking answers for the bleak universe we find ourselves continually sifting through to try and understand the meaning of our time. They spoke gracefully on the intricacy of line work and color construction one evening over rosé, and I knew then I would have to turn to Kandinsky and his exploration of the triangular relationship webbed between artists. I, too, found myself in the triangular configuration when engaging in this project. His writing appears as amethyst-colored text.

Keats' Letters "18 April 1817," "22 November 1817," "27 February 1818," & "22 December 1818" // Pomegranate-Colored Text

When I was attending the Sewanee School of Letters' MFA program studying the craft of Ekphrastic Poetry under Tiana Clark, we studied Keats' "Ode to a Grecian Urn" during one of our early lessons, and I realized then I was being called into Keats' realm. Again, wanting to play with the triangular artistic relationship, Eliot is the tarot mystic, and Keats becomes the mystic of ekphrasis. Pulling from his letters to ground the reader in poetic imagination and wonderment, his lettering appears in pomegranate-colored text.

The Pictorial Key to The Tarot: Being Fragments of a Secret Tradition Under the Veil of Divination by Arthur Arnold Waite & The Tarot of the Bohemians: The Most Ancient Book in the World, for the Use of Initiates by Papus, translated by A.P Morton with the preface written by A.E. Waite // Fern-Colored Text

I had very little knowledge of the art of card reading as divination and fortunetelling but felt drawn to the subject when Theo gifted me a deck of cards. (I later learned there is magic in being given a deck, and my deck was gifted to me by the mythmaker themself... perhaps the magic was born in that moment.) No matter how divine my fascination, I still had to learn the practice. This is what brought me to discovering Waite. While reading the essay, "Eliot and the Tarot" by Robert Currie, I discovered Waite's *Pictorial Key to the Tarot* was likely the same text Eliot was influenced by when constructing the Tarot sections of "The Waste Land." I considered using *The Golden Bough* by James George Frazer, which is widely known to be central to understanding Eliot until I found *The Tarot of the Bohemians*. I feel this text brought a take on ancient magic but in the language of a Modernist that would complete the research I needed to effectively give voice to the ekphrastic divination process. Both of Waite's works appear in fern-colored text.

"The Waste land" by T. S. Eliot & "Eliot and the Tarot" by Robert Currie // Blood-Colored Text

I find it humorous that this research brought me to Eliot, given I have been trying to ignore him for years, but I had to follow the path the cards laid for me to follow. I wanted to credit Robert Currie for bringing me to "The

Waste Land" with fresh eyes and played with his phrasing and shaping of this project with the directness Eliot used in the "The Waste Land." Eliot's poetics quoted in this collection appear in blood-colored text.

"…because you want contact with something greater than yourself and you have questions, and you want the cards to answer you. The problem comes when they do."

—Alexander Chee, "The Querent"

"…there are no grounds for establishing a discourse, but rather an arid millennial ground to break, what I say has at least two sides and two aims: to up, to destroy; and to foresee the unforeseeable"

—Hélène Cixous, "The Laugh of the Medusa"

"It was in that hour that I became negatively capable. My life spiraled onward, and duende became my claim to an errant power."

—Diane Seuss, "I Know You Know"

EKPHRASIS AS DIVINATION
AN INCANTATION CATALOGUE

Your first reading.

Before We Were Learned We Were Magic When We were Magic

Follow me in thought, dear reader,
the human brain acts in accordance
with a very small number of laws,
and the inventor cannot escape
from the effect of this rule.

We come after thinking in moon blues,
sun red, warm and comfortable, until
a weightless pain reminds us
everything is like being birthed.
Submerged with one leg floating beyond
the length of our vertical stretch to touch
the edifice of our thesis and the sand
beyond our reach at present.

Over our head broods symbols
that sometimes look like math
-ematic gifts to aid in our attaining
the maps for our futures,
blending reason with satisfaction.

Here is where we renounce consequences.
Consider the cards:

Our strength resides in contemplation.
Higher meanings are matters of inference
because people aren't always as simple
as the grocery store. Our actions
don't just pop into existence like apples
and bread. We know their work
expresses an internal truth,
that all language is an external form
of children questioning what we see.

A mouthless language fluid as water
from great ewers, irrigating a never-ending
extent of red sunlight or shadow,
standing in water, lying on the grass.
Still sometimes, even the priest does not believe.

Poetry is the failed & beautiful expression
of things that are unnamed.

Nevertheless, we know
the window frames this work's
wicked pack of cards.

Here, said she, is your card,
the view still remains to be written.

Your Second Reading.

What if All I Write and Read is a Nothing and I am a Nothing Too?

It happened long ago. At the violet hour,
when the eyes and back breathed in deep
and bellowed "Sun," they were dried bodies
naked on the ground. Rattled by bones
cast in dry garret, year to year—lost the human engine
though blind & throbbing between two lives.

At the violet hour, the evening hour that strives
homeward and brings a never-ending extent of red;
realizing that to set this red in a careful landscape
would create a discord as to produce appeal

and coherence. To lift their spirits, the story
was told as a hazy landscape around the stream.
They became enraptured with this tale, added to it,
felt over speculations and surmises like the natural Sun.
Natural to them—shined over them
with sober magnificence & soon they forgot
they were lost.

I find that I cannot exist as I look into another
youthful figure looking intently at scholarship,
prodigality, & dissipation.

The path of those who dig the earth says,
The undevout Archeologist is mad.
The plain man says, *Genius is mad.*

O mysterious priest! O archeologist!
The highest meaning lies deeper than language,
picture, or hieroglyph, so I set up camp.

The Archaeologist had been wandering for a long time.
He carried me home in the pack on his back
like I carry my unwritten books.

In poetry—there are very few Axioms,
and soon I will see how far I am from their Centre
as I taper least in the dark my spark. Still—

genius might be the zealous and all-searching mind,
I will wonder at his back from time to time,
who am I coming to sacrifice?

This first book of Nothing looms
over the stacks with nothing.
The development of synthetic symbolism.

We cannot connect the broken fingernails
to our dirty hands. Our people,
humble people, who expect Nothing

from genius, treat the earth
and mountains like stories
of our metallic botany's phenomena

or the animate création of man.
We had never seen before.
And so we made a gesture

with our hands holding a cup,
from which streams poured
waters, descended to place the Word

in the dew of water
spilling metallic black ink
all over these pages.

Your third reading.

Reminiscing Over the Sea

In the beginning there was nothing,
and then there was a word   *water.*
Where the stream met the sea, waves crest
onto memory's shore, but now seems motionless,
or even to move down and backwards.
In the psychic sphere, colour is a power
which directly influences the water's deluge
of the blue distance before the tide
& the expanse of sky which spreads
to the very verge of the Sea. Here some fishermen's
huts are now perched midway & suddenly home
means something it never meant before.
Water, or the passage in Lear that reads—
Do you not hear the Sea? haunts now intensely.

I am fishing in the dull canal on a winter
evening round behind the violet-green
treeshadows. Light dispersing
into fragments, I wade into the water.

The pleasant green smell that fills the forest
is replaced and The First says to me,
Yes, I am your Mother; and The Second
says to me, *Yes, I am your Father.*

It is this first lie that creates the whole universe.
I am the first to hear the thunder beginning
& become intoxicated with light and atmosphere.
I see nothing but pleasant wonders,
and think of delaying here, forever in delight:

We soon forgot we were lost
as we spoke this new world for ourselves.

However, breathing our dream's
difficulty to detail and illustrate

descriptions as tremendous as one
sharpening one's vision into the heart

& nature of Man   of convincing one's nerves
that the World is full of Misery and Heartbreak,
& then so easy did the conquest of art appear.

A Dictionary—turned our words to stones,
but water moved around them & expanded.

Whenever we write, say a Word
or two on some Passage, we find that

we cannot exist without poetry—
That is something that no creation
story will tell us without relying on poetry.

Your fourth reading.

BORN TO A CAHL:
Exploring Our Animalselves

If ever they made a mistake, the river and the trees would bend
beneath the weight, though they still weren't allowed to feel their

animal*selves* until their eyes were properly broken in.
They rarely understood that their existential dilemmas resulted

from a problem with something as paltry as clothing.
Cat and wolf fear the natural mind in the presence

of that place of exit when there is only reflected light
to guide it—one foot upon the earth and one upon waters:

Here they are in cats' alley where the dead
are as lost as bones.

She is all things universal message which has been given to man by woman; she does herself carry its interpretation. the card signifies the door or gate by which an entrance is obtained into this life, the Garden which is the secret known by her

Drawn from things above,
derived to things below.

Our strong, intensive interest disappears,
various properties of flame are balanced.
In this way, the whole world becomes
gradually disenchanted.

When we realize that trees give shade,
that horses run fast and motor-cars still faster,
that cats bite, that the figure seen in a mirror
is not a real human being but light:

drawn from things above
derived to things below

Vermillion has the charm of flame,
which has always attracted human hurt.
The eye, in time, as a prolonged,
shrill trumpet-note for the ear,
and we, the gazers, turn away to seek relief

                                      in blue or green.

Your fifth reading.

BE CAREFUL WHAT YOU READ:
WE TINKER WITH SIGHT AS SEEING

Imagine Adam's dream—

They saw a perfect face, a young woman's,
with eyes closed & a secretive smile. She whispered
to them and saw a word unfold and become

a myriad of smaller words. They saw the letters
of those words break and reform and then saw—
the Pattern   a higher allegory   a symbol

of secrets curiously veiled. When they awoke, they found
they were zealous in this affair because they were never
able to perceive any thing as a known truth
other than questions like:

Do you mean to tell me that you wrote NOTHING?
You spent all your time on shore cataloging LEAVES?

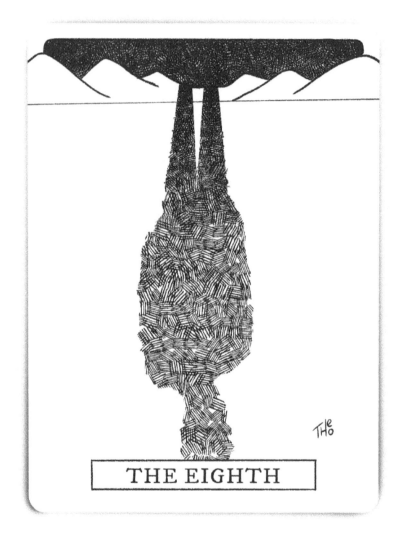

The whole forest became a muffled silence
—birds stopped singing & next came fear
that tingled in the marrow. The earthy smell
of the forest turned sickly as though demanding,
Get him!   the tree   waited.
The forest filled with the sound of tearing roots.
We saw that none of the symbols changed, the words.
A man hung by foot, resting between mountains,
each bearing branches which have been cut off.
It felt as though something were being torn
within his bone; it echoed loud in the silence
of the tree. The man's hands were tied
behind his back. His eyes were the wind.
After the tearing stopped, he remained
in the tree and turned white as a Garden of bones.

Why is there horror in mythmaking?
Because The Tinker made the gun to kill.

Rather than hunger as we do,
delight in the sensation
after Truth. Adam's dream again
will have to do here:

Shadow of reality to come—a fruit of any kind,
all things are produced like we are produced
as the image of individual and corporeal existence.
With fine suddenness—compare great things with small—
have we ever been surprised within a delicious place—
by a delicious voice, a steaming mug of mulled cider,
rabbit stew, and smoked fish?

This is the talent of artists; the organic form
falls into the background; the abstract ideal
achieves greater prominence but also
the talent of us who eat this poisoned fruit.

Your sixth reading.

Pain is What Doubles Joy

The night of the spirit falls darkly.
Deeper becomes the misery
of blind and terrified guides, tormented
& unnerved by fear & doubt.

This gradual darkening—the final
sudden leap into the formless landscape—
where the tree staves planted
in the foreground reveal
a figure whose meaning remains
unaltered. Imagine it is [   ]

I am continually running away from subject—
the case of a complex Mind—one that is imaginative
and at the same time careful of its fruits—
years should bring the philosophic Mind—
antiquities playing cards, the school of vulgar divination,
working on the traditional lines of printed books.
This art, my art, is the child of its age

and the mother of my emotions.

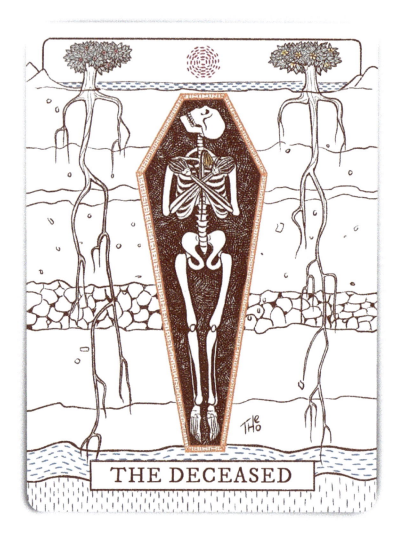

Art is its intensity. More correctly,
a question of analogy. One is concerned
with the fall   into the animal state,
a House of Falsehood illustrates the most
comprehensive way   to an old truth:
What is within us which does sound a trumpet?
Does all that is lower in our nature rise in response?
Almost a moment. Almost in the twinkling of an eye.
The dead in us fail to rise from their tombs knowing:

We hate poetry—Pain, Sickness, and Oppression
We are in a Mist—the burden of the Mystery,
We feel we are now in that state, and still someday,
we too shall explore those dark Passages.

Your seventh reading.

When Someone Told Me a Joke
Years Before I Started Listening

The moon pours down influences
destroying the old convention
that it is sane to be an artist.
Between the world yawns a gulf
which few can cross, so I imagine
the act of flying & discover the dead land
looks like Lilacs scattered out stirring
with the roots of desire.

If I libel my own muse as a relic
of the day, dull memories still pursue
for a butterfly winging its way cannot
grow to be a moth, & I cannot occupy
paradise or an Earthly body with a serpent
twining round my neck for the world.

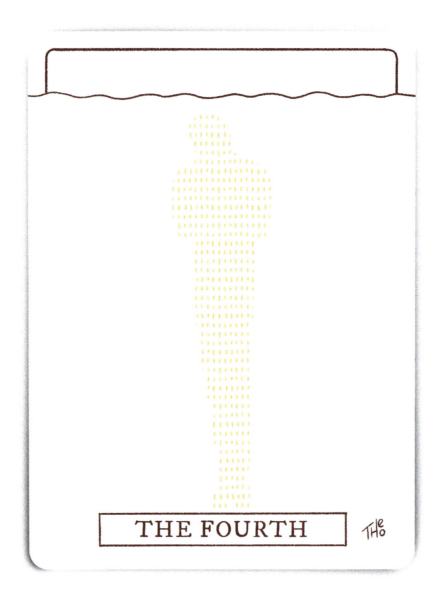

The veil or mask   perpetuates change
from lower   to higher and this is more fitly
represented & rectified   as these apocalyptic visions.
If I should die,   said I to myself
is a crude notion   my reaping skeleton knows,
I have left   *no immortal work behind me—*
nothing   which signifies life
just the inner   work is impossible
to make my friends proud   of my memory.
Crude notion of the reaping   skeleton & spectator
exchange a reality   for a blind dreamland
where truth's inner feeling can   & cannot be felt
while prelate clasped hands   awaits our end.
A crude notion reaps   our skeletons again
& again & again   to rattle our buried abandoned bones.

I have just written my own muse,
and she tells me not to be uneasy
about arbitrary Letters, Eccentricity,
& manner.

This is simply the card of human love.
Here you are, she says, *and who might you be?*
with a warm greeting between vice and virtue.

Don't worry, she laughs and closes her eyes
and fits her hands around her own neck.
In a sense, this card is a mystery.
A change in the form of consciousness:

Just don't tell, she says with a wink, *It will be
our secret. Now comes the real show!*

Your eighth reading.

I DID DO A DIVINATION READING FOR MYSELF:
Death, Corporeal Life, and Destiny

This Threshold is reached by many artificial paths:
hash, narcotics, hypnotics of every kind,
for the practices of spiritual mediums.

They must develop a method by which they shape
patterns and create individual parts
then knit the parts together to create

a working whole. Their writings are still
instrumental in the development of Magic,
though they could not see how the study

of Magic could somehow help Magic
atone for its sins and mend the way
that it has broken the world.

The library is just another large Mansion
of Many Apartments. Now kept shut
with a lock & contains only one book.

They add to this book from time to time,
but otherwise, don't open its covers,
much like the doors of the rest remain shut up.

The River is my nebulous in-between
& speaks to my question about good things—

After eating and drinking a lot of wine,
I realize my sopping wet notes
are what I found in the bottom of bottles.
I drink this old Wine of Heaven
because I am told it is necessary
for eternal Happiness, though still
the key has not yet been revealed to me.

This skill is not easy to develop.
Every time I fill a journal
& manipulate the underlying patterns of things,
my clever eye for external observation
helps me figure out the purposes of patterns,
which I realize is only the redigestion of Musings
but also an increased knowledge of things.

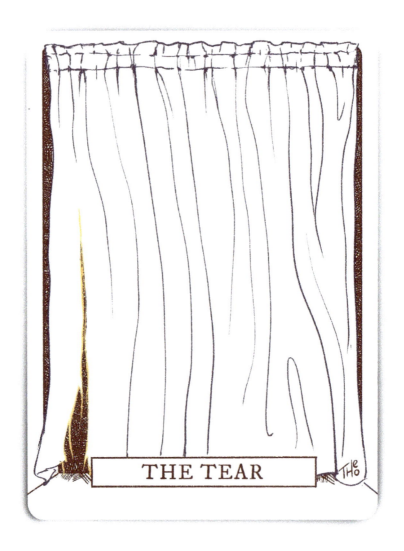

Why should we kick against the Pricks

when we can walk on Roses?

Why should we be Eagles, when we can be Owls?
Why if we should forget to announce the coming end

of the game, will all the spectators have a right
to share in our naming? Fortunetelling

should be great & unobtrusive,
a thing which enters into one's soul

and does not startle it or amaze it
with itself but with its subject,

but woe to him who attempts to pass it before
long and laborious preliminary preparation.

Your ninth reading.

Ode to Writing Divinatory Meanings

I do not look through her glass.
I do not look through her laurel crown.
I look to just see her, and when finally
I see her, I realize the foolish milliner's
countenance is full of intelligence and dream.

Between two dangers, like waking sickness.
Over time, tastes changes and belly swells.
So do her feet and her hands,
every part of her mind finding—language.
Words become her ever-pregnant dreams.

What is happening to me? cries this card,
which is blank, but still something she carries,
which we are forbidden to see
because I still do not find words.

Borrow a Botanical Dictionary—turn to the words.
Now your hands are grasping a cloud, a bit of folded
birch bark layered with scribble but not without reason.

The white space is taken as symbolizing
spotless purity and black ink grief
because it's where meaning is written.

A blend of black and white turns the words
silent and motionless, composed of grief and death,
which draws circles like crowns of Laurel and Prunus

& begs you to show the explanations
to your sisters. Divinatory Meanings:
Triumph, the excessive degree in everything,

is conquest concurred through naming,
sharing reality and continual help,
which values a kind dictionary.

Modern artists are beginning to realize
they are the spiritual teachers of the world,
and for their teaching to have weight,
it must be comprehensible—
like a dark, cloaked figure,
like a sculptor in a monastery,
or like a human being sits holding a
book
& turns over the pages with a
thoughtful aspect,
but their actions have for them no
meaning.

I bring the horoscope myself,
a design which illustrates:

something I am not ready to
name.

Your tenth reading

What is Beneath / What is Behind / What is Before

They obey Socrates' command—Know thyself.
Consciously or unconsciously the artist
with a globe on their head, another shade
of red—running blood is studying and proving
their material, setting in balanced spiritual values:

> *The Root and the flower*
> *read as one card in two phases*
> *behind and before*

This dual sign is   drawn from things above and
  below.   the symbols
signifying   natural life,   lie like   roses and lilies
         changed into garden flowers,
        the divine motive   man reflecting
God,   is
also the unity of individual being   and
 thought,   leaning on
       a clump of greenery   one
would say that these were   treasures   .

We realized then that the world
had gone completely silent,
each scratch felt as though it were
etched into our skull:

> *The Root and the flower,*
> *read as one card in two phases*
> *behind and before*

The proper meanings of this card
are rooted in doctrine.

Your eleventh reading.

Because Their Eyes are Closed

I wrote last of a general weakness
of the whole system from an anxiety.
A nagging sense, like an itch
in the back of my head.

I sat on a stump and pulled out:
a list, a spool of thread,
an assortment of buttons,
a candle to let me see this blood, a needle,
& scraps of pages I tore from books I found
too heavy to carry.

I just needed to calm down.
Focus on one thing at a time.
Surely, I could get it all by the end.
My face, a calmness of countenance
that I can never forget, said
What is Divinatory Meaning?

It is an intimation of that which may lie
behind the House of the heart, joy, content,
nourishment, abundance, fertile **phraseology**.
I know the colour of that blood—it is arterial
blood—I cannot be deceived in that colour.
That drop of blood is a death-warrant.

Near the Delta where the stream met the sea,
the rain fell in a pattern & formed a rhythm
seeking reward for this dexterity, power
of vision and experience. My purpose became
the satisfaction of vanity and greed. Restless
and muttering "stream," you and I drifted together
down from the source & waited for rain,
while the black clouds gathered far—the sun
spoke into the sky & disappeared behind the mountains,
& now you and I rest as the water pools
into a great sea again.

Why will you go out in this weather?
I fatigue myself with writing
too much about the sea's stories
& wreckage.

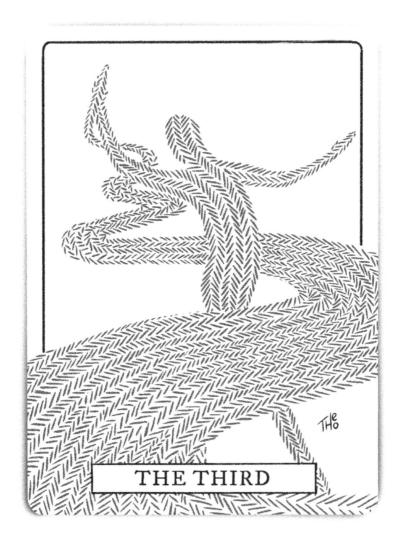

Still, we are hiding behind our stoic glare.
Slowly we lift our now empty lunar crescent
at our feet, a horned diadem surrounds us,
and a large solar crosses on our breast.
We turn our body to leave.

We walk deliberately through the open door
and turn the corner into the hallway.
There is a Shekinah both above and below.
As soon as we were out of sight, we ran
as quietly as we can out of this cage.

We will not sing in a cage.
We will be as obstinate as Robins—singular and plural.
These fragments I have shored against my ruins..
We are a thousand of them, my dearest.

Your last reading.

HER HOUSE:
Another Signifier

Every word spoken rouses inner vibrations.
Every object represents the subject
& then becomes a thing. The artist will be called to
natural form and colour. And if they
neglect this thing that ought not to be neglected,
they will deprive themselves of this possibility
& limit their powers of expression—Madame Wade,
child of our age, mother of our emotions
that pool like water into a great sea
from an ancient body of stories long
& never printed.

We come now to the final practical part,
a field guide to a mythical country
that has always lived parallel to our own.
A building divided into many rooms
may be large or small, designed by Hall
ways before our journey. Every wall
of every room is pictures; perhaps they number
a thousand cards. The way to consult
and obtain our musings on divinatory art,
the mysteries of light—persons versed
in questions believe the way of simplicity
is the way of truth:

This is how you tie an apron.
And so, the ritual was born.

Artists are in every segment.
We can see beyond segments.
By listening, we can understand when
the prophet proclaims: a *Spiritual life
is like swimming.*

We topple off the bank into the water,
 & if we do not strive tirelessly,
do not fight continually against sinking,
we will go under.

Still in the wake of waves we hear
our voice like honey
but more sincere.

Epilogue,
or Instructions on How to Reread This Collection should you Choose:

1. Close your eyes and walk out of your reading—you may have lost yourself, but you will find the edge of your shadow still combing through the blades of grass.

2. Let yourself be silent as you blur into the card's language that fractures like light through a prism.

3. Return to the cards, find your meaning in them, arrange them differently if you like, untether them from their binding, cut them into halves and make them a new journey. Altogether they're meaningless but free of the constellations you use to make meaning.

4. This work was written to be destroyed.

5. Don't reread to conquer them—read to feel the language, familiar word making. You'll know it when you are doing it, because you are no longer trying to burn your own image onto the page. You'll soon realize that your image was always there, behind the text—it's that until now, maybe, no one was pointing to you.

6. Look around you—are you ever alone?

7. Look past the colors in the cards—let them bleed, let them dance, let them live.

8. Make notations in the margins. Between your marginalia and the poems is where the real work is written.

9. Poetry is meant to be a lived sanctuary. Poetry is destroyed by inked permanence. Poetry is benumbed when left abandoned in a closed book forever. It's okay if you think of yourself as a living poem. It's okay if you think the poem is dust. In the end, the poem gets to just be poemed.

10. Read something beautiful before returning to your divinations. We all need to remember to read something beautiful during the day.

11. These fortunes might destroy you if you cage them tightly.

12. Know that none of these writings are about you—know that all these readings are about you—know that I am you. Know that you are me too.

13. Read something difficult between your divination readings to remind you that no matter how much you search, you are never finished searching, that the only truth we are gifted is between the pages as we turn them over and over and over and over again.

14. Don't believe the cards because they distort their meanings to hurt you.

15. Trust what you are searching for—it chose you.

16. When you return to your subject, let go of what you already discovered. Let yourself find something to renew.

17. Don't distrust the cards. They long to be true like you long to just be.

18. If you found meaning in your reading, you were reading these poems correctly. If you did not find meaning in your reading, you were reading these poems correctly.

19. Try to remember your birth before returning to them. Remember the blood that baptized you, the opal hollow of your young eyes searching for your mother while you were bathed in isolating light, the air pulsing against your skin for the first time—and know that is how you should reread this work.

20. The poems you read here are not mine but found through the exploration of many mouths—mouths loud with teeth that bite.

21. Did you hear the music? If not, keep listening. It will find you when you are ready.

22. Have you felt so good to get to the meaning of poems? Stop that shit and just let yourself be.

23. Don't ask too many questions—you felt the answers but have been taught not to trust that you can feel them. We all just want to trust, friend.

24. In mythmaking, there is always an element of horror. Remember that when you return.

25. Find a room without corners to read in, so you can find a place to hide in the corners of the cards.

26. When you are reading them, you become a mythmaker—journey within the three through the dark Hallways that exist inside you. Wade into meaning like a child who is learning to swim. Learn, leer, linger if you haven't already.

27. Did you see your card?

28. Don't be afraid to laugh at them, pain often doubles joy. But when you reread, look for laughter, so you see your own joy this time.

29. If you hate this work when you are finished, bury it in your backyard and watch the grass grow over the mound—soil erases permanence, native foliage hides the scar.

30. If you like this work, hide it from yourself so you can forget it or give it away to a stranger in a bar who is between too few and too many. If they return it, reread it. If they don't, let go of searching for a season.

31. Know that I know, that you know, that we know, there is something captured by ink spills that language will always be chasing. Know that I know, that you know, that we know that there is always something blood is mute too—that anxiety is an anxiety we have to live in.

32. Trust your haunts—those ghosts know you better than you want to see—they may even be who brought you to pulling this text from the endless ocean of texts we all swim.

33. Don't lose yourself entirely in the cards because there are narratives yet to be discovered here. What if you were meant to make the map for us to follow?

34. Be still and know that your relic is the relic of these cards.

35. We will never be finished.

Acknowledgments

This collection would not have been written without the diligent eye of Tiana Clark, and her showing me Robin Coste Lewis's collection *Voyage of the Sable Venus and other Poems*. Both Lewis's collection and Clark loosened me from my binding and set the pages of me to drift out over an endless sea of cards. Nickole Brown for her gently showing me how beautiful a sentence can be. Justin Taylor for believing in this work and advising me on how to navigate how it felt once I turned it over to the world.

To Diane Seuss who taught me how to use my wall of sound without hiding behind my own hurt. Her friendship changed my life, and I hope when she reads the Epilogue and arrives at number nine, she sees that I have hidden her name within another list. Thank you for everything, Di.

To Michelle Castleberry, Marie Kressin, and Anna Konradi for their sisterhood. When we sat outside the Sewanee Inn and ate a delicious meal none of us could afford, drank cocktails while Michelle drew our cards and we cried through laughing. I will hold them all and that night as inspiration deep in my belly for years and years to come. I love you.

To Shawn Choquette-Brown who sat on the couch with me and told me, "not that line," "what the hell are you trying to say here?" and "damn! That's the one" while I wrote this work. You are my family. To Donald, Mary, Mom and Dad for exposing me to the rich world beyond my own path. You are in all the works I write. Lance Ummenhofer, my partner in this life, thank you for believing in me, in us, when I struggle to—I love you more everyday and will continuously be in awe of your way with words.

To my Turney Center and Riverbend Students because they reminded me of the importance of poetry during times when people need it most. Y'all are all living poems to me.

To everyone at April Gloaming, the Free Nashville Poetry Library, and Humble Universe Books because together we are writing and curating an American South that tells the story unslanted. Their dedication to fostering literary spaces and community during a time when that community is being attacked and books banned is why I will never be able to thank them enough.

Huge thanks to Unsolicited Press for taking a leap of faith and publishing this wicked little book.

To the trouts that swim in an endless river wanting to conform when they should be longing to swim and let creatives be.

To one of the early readers of this work who reminded me of how intelligent I am, I hope he feels changed now, but if I am being honest, I don't really give a shit if he does, and he seems too simple to be, anyway.

And lastly, William Faulkner's ghost, because when this book is printed in colored text, I know he will understand why the words had to be printed in color.

About the Makers Behind this Collection

Theo Hall // Myth Maker:

When Theo Hall was a child, they hoped they would grow up to be a prophet who could hear the voice of God. Unfortunately, God wasn't all that chatty, so they became an artist and designer instead. They started creating the *Young World* mythology in 2008 in their childhood bedroom and have slowly built it bit-by-bit in bedrooms and living rooms and coffeeshops ever since. They have written *Young World* short stories, created a deck of *Young World* cards, fabricated several *Young World* artifacts, and workshopped a live *Young World* storytelling show complete with original music and costuming at open mics in Metro Detroit. When not slowly picking away at a massive project that has only been seen by about 10 people, they do graphic design for nonprofits, small businesses, and artists.

Meg Wade // Prophet Poetess:

Meg Wade is a National Poetry Series finalist and a former Diane Middlebrook Poetry Fellow at the University of Wisconsin's Creative Writing Institute. Her chapbook, *Slick Like Dark,* won the 2017 Tupelo Press Snowbound Chapbook Award and is now available from Tupelo Press. Meg has been the recipient of an Academy of American Poets Prize and is Curator and Founder of Be Witched, a literary and arts event series.

She lives and writes in Nashville, Tennessee. Meg grew up in the foothills of the Smoky Mountains. She is the last in the long line of Appalachian Granny Witches in her family. Her spiritual practices belong to a closed culture.

Robyn Leigh Lear // Poetic Medium:

Robyn Leigh Lear is a poet, Creative Director for April Gloaming Publishing, and an Associate Professor currently teaching in Nashville, TN. Lear's forthcoming manuscript, *Ekphrasis as Divination: An Incantation Catalogue* (Unsolicited Press, February 2025) engages in found language and ekphrasis to explore the divinatory cards designed by artist Theo Hall (they/them). She is currently finalizing her second manuscript, *Yonderling*, written under the mentorship of Diane Seuss, which explores the binary of place and self, framed by what she terms "the violent pastoral." She is currently an MFA candidate in poetry at the University of the South, and her poetry was recently selected for the Kindling Arts Festival and has appeared in *Wild Roof Journal* and *Grand Little Things*.

About the Press

Unsolicited Press is based out of Portland, Oregon and focuses on the works of the unsung and underrepresented. As a womxn-owned, all-volunteer small publisher that doesn't worry about profits as much as championing exceptional literature, we have the privilege of partnering with authors skirting the fringes of the lit world. We've worked with emerging and award-winning authors such as Amy Shimshon-Santo, Brook Bhagat, Elisa Carlsen, Tara Stillions Whitehead, and Anne Leigh Parrish.

Learn more at unsolicitedpress.com. Find us on Instagram, X, Facebook, Pinterest, Bsky, Threads, YouTube, and LinkedIn. Unsolicited Press also writes a snarky newsletter on Substack.

www.ingramcontent.com/pod-product-compliance
Lightning Source LLC
LaVergne TN
LVHW052131210525
811938LV00040B/809